# The Message
# of Christmas

## Eugene H. Peterson

**NAVPRESS**

BRINGING TRUTH TO LIFE

P.O. Box 35001, Colorado Springs, Colorado 80935

Old Testament Exegetical
Consultants:
Prof. Donald R. Glenn
  Dallas Theological Seminary
Dr. Tremper Longman III
  Westmont College
Dr. John N. Oswalt
  Wesley Biblical Seminary

New Testament Exegetical
Consultants:
Dr. William W. Klein
  Denver Seminary
Dr. Darrell L. Bock
  Dallas Theological Seminary
Dr. Moisés Silva
  Gordon-Conwell Theologi-
  cal Seminary
The Rev. Dr. Rodney A.
  Whitacre
  Trinity Episcopal School of
  Ministry

Published in association with the literary agency of Alive
Communications, 7680 Goddard Street, Ste. 200, Colorado
Springs, CO 80920.

Cover art: "Starry Night" by Vincent Van Gogh

ISBN 1-57683-265-1

Printed in the United States of America

2 3 4 5 6 7 8 9 10 11 12 13 14 15 / 05 04 03 02 01

# Christmas

The story of Jesus' birth has an immense progeny. Our planet fairly teems with stories and songs, paintings and drama that got their start from this story. The reproductive energies show no sign of tapering off. Writers and singers and artists, to say nothing of countless children and parents and grandparents all over the world, continue to find fresh and novel ways of keeping this story going.

But even more impressive are the lives that continue to get a fresh start—a new birth—in the story of this birth. Day after day, men and women who feel more dead than alive, in the hearing or singing or seeing of this story rediscover the utter and unspeakable and beautiful preciousness of life. The story of Jesus' birth gets reproduced in these human lives still, over and over and over again.

The birth of Jesus is a birth with a message. It takes the entire Bible to bring the complete message, but this birth is the core of it: In Jesus, God is here to give us life, real life.

# A Savior Foretold

# A Righteous Branch

*Jeremiah 23:5-6*

"Time's coming" —GOD's Decree—
>  "when I'll establish a truly righteous David
>      Branch,
A ruler who knows how to rule justly.
>      He'll make sure of justice and keep people
>          united.
In his time Judah will be secure again
>      and Israel will live in safety.
This is the name they'll give him:
>      'GOD-Who-Puts-Everything-Right.'"

# A Child Will Be Born to Us

*Isaiah 9:2-7*

The people who walked in darkness
>      have seen a great light.
For those who lived in a land of deep shadows—
>      light! Sunbursts of light!
You repopulated the nation,
>      you expanded its joy.
Oh, they're so glad in your presence!
>      Festival joy!

The joy of a great celebration,
    sharing rich gifts and warm greetings.
The abuse of oppressors and cruelty of tyrants—
    all their whips and cudgels and curses—
Is gone, done away with, a deliverance
    as surprising and sudden as Gideon's old
        victory over Midian.
The boots of all those invading troops,
    along with their shirts soaked with innocent
        blood,
Will be piled in a heap and burned,
    a fire that will burn for days!
For a child has been born—for us!
    the gift of a son—for us!
He'll take over
    the running of the world.
His names will be: Amazing Counselor,
    Strong God,
Eternal Father,
    Prince of Wholeness.
His ruling authority will grow,
    and there'll be no limits to the wholeness he
        brings.

# A Righteous Judge

*Isaiah 11:1-5*

A green Shoot will sprout from Jesse's stump,
    from his roots a budding Branch.
The life-giving Spirit of GOD will hover over him,
    the Spirit that brings wisdom and
        understanding,
The Spirit that gives direction and builds strength,
    the Spirit that instills knowledge and Fear-of-
        GOD.
Fear-of-GOD
    will be all his joy and delight.
    He won't judge by appearances, won't decide
        on the basis of hearsay.
He'll judge the needy by what is right,
    render decisions on earth's poor with justice.
His words will bring everyone to awed attention.
    A mere breath from his lips will topple the
        wicked.
Each morning he'll pull on sturdy work clothes
        and boots,
    and build righteousness and faithfulness in
        the land.

# Behold My Chosen One

*Isaiah 42:1-4*

"Take a good look at my servant.
  I'm backing him to the hilt.
He's the one I chose,
  and I couldn't be more pleased with him.
I've bathed him with my Spirit, my *life*.
  He'll set everything right among the nations.
He won't call attention to what he does
  with loud speeches or gaudy parades.
He won't brush aside the bruised and the hurt
  and he won't disregard the small and
      insignificant,
  but he'll steadily and firmly set things right.
He won't tire out and quit. He won't be stopped
  until he's finished his work—to set things
      right on earth.
Far-flung ocean islands
  wait expectantly for his teaching."

## Your King Is Coming

*Zechariah 9:9-10*

"Shout and cheer, Daughter Zion!
    Raise the roof, Daughter Jerusalem!
Your king is coming!
    a good king who makes all things right,
    a humble king riding a donkey,
    a mere colt of a donkey.
I've had it with war—no more chariots in
        Ephraim,
    no more war horses in Jerusalem,
    no more swords and spears, bows and arrows.
He will offer peace to the nations,
    a peaceful rule worldwide,
    from the four winds to the seven seas."


## A Virgin With Child

*Isaiah 7:10-14*

GOD spoke again to Ahaz. This time he said, "Ask
for a sign from your GOD. Ask anything. Be
extravagant. Ask for the moon!"

But Ahaz said, "I'd never do that. I'd never
make demands like that on God!"

So Isaiah told him, "Then listen to this,
government of David! It's bad enough that you
make people tired with your pious, timid
hypocrisies, but now you're making God tired.
So the Master is going to give you a sign anyway.
Watch for this: A girl who is presently a virgin will
get pregnant. She'll bear a son and name him
Immanuel ["God-With-Us"]."

## The Announcement to Mary

*Luke 1:26-38*

God sent the angel Gabriel to the Galilean village
of Nazareth to a virgin engaged to be married to a
man descended from David. His name was Joseph,
and the virgin's name, Mary. Upon entering,
Gabriel greeted her:

> "Good morning!
> You're beautiful with God's beauty,
> Beautiful inside and out!
> God be with you."

She was thoroughly shaken, wondering what
was behind a greeting like that. But the angel
assured her, "Mary, you have nothing to fear. God
has a surprise for you: You will become pregnant
and give birth to a son and call his name Jesus.

"He will be great,
be called 'Son of the Highest.'
The Lord God will give him
the throne of his father David;
He will rule Jacob's house forever—
no end, ever, to his kingdom."

Mary said to the angel, "But how? I've never slept with a man."

The angel answered,

"The Holy Spirit will come upon you,
the power of the Highest hover over you;
Therefore, the child you bring to birth
will be called Holy, Son of God.

"And did you know that your cousin Elizabeth conceived a son, old as she is? Everyone called her barren, and here she is six months pregnant! Nothing, you see, is impossible with God."

And Mary said,

"Yes, I see it all now:
I'm the Lord's maid, ready to serve.
Let it be with me
just as you say."

Then the angel left her.

# Elizabeth and Mary

## Luke 1:39-56

Mary didn't waste a minute. She got up and
traveled to a town in Judah in the hill country,
straight to Zachariah's house, and greeted
Elizabeth. When Elizabeth heard Mary's greeting,
the baby in her womb leaped. She was filled with
the Holy Spirit, and sang out exuberantly,

> "You're so blessed among women,
>> and the babe in your womb, also blessed!
> And why am I so blessed that
>> the mother of my Lord visits me?
> The moment the sound of your
>> greeting entered my ears,
> The babe in my womb
>> skipped like a lamb for sheer joy.
> Blessed woman, who believed what God said,
>> believed every word would come true!"

And Mary said,

> "I'm bursting with God-news;
>> I'm dancing the song of my Savior God.
> God took one good look at me, and look
>> what happened—
> I'm the most fortunate woman on earth!

What God has done for me will never be
        forgotten,
    the God whose very name is holy, set apart
        from all others.
His mercy flows in wave after wave
    on those who are in awe before him.
He bared his arm and showed his strength,
    scattered the bluffing braggarts.
He knocked tyrants off their high horses,
    pulled victims out of the mud.
The starving poor sat down to a banquet;
    the callous rich were left out in the cold.
He embraced his chosen child, Israel;
    he remembered and piled on the mercies,
        piled them high.
It's exactly what he promised,
    beginning with Abraham and right up to
        now."

Mary stayed with Elizabeth for three months
and then went back to her own home.

# A Savior Is Born

# The Birth

### *Matthew 1:18-25*

The birth of Jesus took place like this. His mother, Mary, was engaged to be married to Joseph. Before they came to the marriage bed, Joseph discovered she was pregnant. (It was by the Holy Spirit, but he didn't know that.) Joseph, chagrined but noble, determined to take care of things quietly so Mary would not be disgraced.

While he was trying to figure a way out, he had a dream. God's angel spoke in the dream: "Joseph, son of David, don't hesitate to get married. Mary's pregnancy is Spirit-conceived. God's Holy Spirit has made her pregnant. She will bring a son to birth, and when she does, you, Joseph, will name him Jesus—'God saves'—because he will save his people from their sins." This would bring the prophet's embryonic sermon to full term:

"Watch for this—a virgin will get pregnant
and bear a son;
They will name him Emmanuel" (Hebrew for
"God is with us").

Then Joseph woke up. He did exactly what God's angel commanded in the dream: He married Mary. But he did not consummate the marriage until she had the baby. He named the baby Jesus.

*Luke 2:1-7*

About that time Caesar Augustus ordered a census to be taken throughout the Empire. This was the first census when Quirinius was governor of Syria. Everyone had to travel to his own ancestral hometown to be accounted for. So Joseph went from the Galilean town of Nazareth up to Bethlehem in Judah, David's town, for the census. As a descendant of David, he had to go there. He went with Mary, his fiancée, who was pregnant.

While they were there, the time came for her to give birth. She gave birth to a son, her firstborn. She wrapped him in a blanket and laid him in a manger, because there was no room in the hostel.

## The Shepherds and Angels Came

*Luke 2:8-20*

There were sheepherders camping in the neighborhood. They had set night watches over their sheep. Suddenly, God's angel stood among them and God's glory blazed around them. They were terrified. The angel said, "Don't be afraid. I'm here to announce a great and joyful event that is meant for everybody, worldwide: A Savior has just been born in David's town, a Savior who is Messiah and Master. This is what you're to look for: a baby wrapped in a blanket and lying in a manger."

At once the angel was joined by a huge angelic choir singing God's praises:

> "Glory to God in the heavenly heights,
> Peace to all men and women on earth who
>      please him."

As the angel choir withdrew into heaven, the sheepherders talked it over. "Let's get over to Bethlehem as fast as we can and see for ourselves what God has revealed to us." They left, running, and found Mary and Joseph, and the baby lying in the manger. Seeing was believing. They told everyone they met what the angels had said about this child. All who heard the sheepherders were impressed.

Mary kept all these things to herself, holding them dear, deep within herself. The sheepherders returned and let loose, glorifying and praising God for everything they had heard and seen. It turned out exactly the way they'd been told!

# Presentation in the Temple

## *Luke 2:21-38*

When the eighth day arrived, the day of circumcision, the child was named Jesus, the name given by the angel before he was conceived.

Then when the days stipulated by Moses for purification were complete, they took him up to Jerusalem to offer him to God as commanded in God's Law: "Every male who opens the womb shall be a holy offering to God," and also to sacrifice the "pair of doves or two young pigeons" prescribed in God's Law.

In Jerusalem at the time, there was a man, Simeon by name, a good man, a man who lived in the prayerful expectancy of help for Israel. And the Holy Spirit was on him. The Holy Spirit had shown him that he would see the Messiah of God before he died. Led by the Spirit, he entered the Temple. As the parents of the child Jesus brought him in to carry out the rituals of the Law, Simeon took him into his arms and blessed God:

"God, you can now release your servant;
    release me in peace as you promised.
With my own eyes I've seen your salvation;
    it's now out in the open for everyone to see:

A God-revealing light to the non-Jewish
nations,
and of glory for your people Israel."

Jesus' father and mother were speechless with surprise at these words. Simeon went on to bless them, and said to Mary his mother,

"This child marks both the failure and
the recovery of many in Israel,
A figure misunderstood and contradicted—
the pain of a sword-thrust through you—
But the rejection will force honesty,
as God reveals who they really are."

Anna the prophetess was also there, a daughter of Phanuel from the tribe of Asher. She was by now a very old woman. She had been married seven years and a widow for eighty-four. She never left the Temple area, worshiping night and day with her fastings and prayers. At the very time Simeon was praying, she showed up, broke into an anthem of praise to God, and talked about the child to all who were waiting expectantly for the freeing of Jerusalem.

# The Visit of the Magi

*Matthew 2:1-12*

After Jesus was born in Bethlehem village, Judah territory—this was during Herod's kingship—a band of scholars arrived in Jerusalem from the East. They asked around, "Where can we find and pay homage to the newborn King of the Jews? We observed a star in the eastern sky that signaled his birth. We're on pilgrimage to worship him."

When word of their inquiry got to Herod, he was terrified—and not Herod alone, but most of Jerusalem as well. Herod lost no time. He gathered all the high priests and religion scholars in the city together and asked, "Where is the Messiah supposed to be born?"

They told him, "Bethlehem, Judah territory. The prophet Micah wrote it plainly:

"'It's you, Bethlehem, in Judah's land,
    no longer bringing up the rear.
From you will come the leader
    who will shepherd-rule my people, my
        Israel.'"

Herod then arranged a secret meeting with the scholars from the East. Pretending to be as devout as they were, he got them to tell him exactly when the birth-announcement star appeared. Then he told them the prophecy about Bethlehem, and said, "Go find this child. Leave no stone unturned. As soon as you find him, send word and I'll join you at once in your worship."

Instructed by the king, they set off. Then the star appeared again, the same star they had seen in the eastern skies. It led them on until it hovered over the place of the child. They could hardly contain themselves: They were in the right place! They had arrived at the right time!

They entered the house and saw the child in the arms of Mary, his mother. Overcome, they kneeled and worshiped him. Then they opened their luggage and presented gifts: gold, frankincense, myrrh.

In a dream, they were warned not to report back to Herod. So they worked out another route, left the territory without being seen, and returned to their own country.

# A Savior Lives On

# The Preeminent Christ

## Colossians 1:15-23

We look at this Son and see the God who cannot
be seen. We look at this Son and see God's
original purpose in everything created. For
everything, absolutely everything, above and
below, visible and invisible, rank after rank after
rank of angels—*everything* got started in him and
finds its purpose in him. He was there before any
of it came into existence and holds it all together
right up to this moment. And when it comes to
the church, he organizes and holds it together, like
a head does a body.

He was supreme in the beginning and—lead-
ing the resurrection parade—he is supreme in the
end. From beginning to end he's there, towering
far above everything, everyone. So spacious is he,
so roomy, that everything of God finds its proper
place in him without crowding. Not only that, but
all the broken and dislocated pieces of the
universe—people and things, animals and
atoms—get properly fixed and fit together in
vibrant harmonies, all because of his death, his
blood that poured down from the Cross.

You yourselves are a case study of what he
does. At one time you all had your backs turned

to God, thinking rebellious thoughts of him, giving him trouble every chance you got. But now, by giving himself completely at the Cross, actually *dying* for you, Christ brought you over to God's side and put your lives together, whole and holy in his presence. You don't walk away from a gift like that! You stay grounded and steady in that bond of trust, constantly tuned in to the Message, careful not to be distracted or diverted. There is no other Message—just this one. Every creature under heaven gets this same Message. I, Paul, am a messenger of this Message.

## Worthy Is the Lamb

### Revelation 5:1-14

I saw a scroll in the right hand of the One Seated on the Throne. It was written on both sides, fastened with seven seals. I also saw a powerful Angel, calling out in a voice like thunder, "Is there anyone who can open the scroll, who can break its seals?"

There was no one—no one in Heaven, no one on earth, no one from the underworld—able to break open the scroll and read it.

I wept and wept and wept that no one was found able to open the scroll, able to read it. One of the Elders said, "Don't weep. Look—the Lion from Tribe Judah, the Root of David's Tree, has conquered. He can open the scroll, can rip through the seven seals."

So I looked, and there, surrounded by Throne, Animals, and Elders, was a Lamb, slaughtered but standing tall. Seven horns he had, and seven eyes, the Seven Spirits of God sent into all the earth. He came to the One Seated on the Throne and took the scroll from his right hand. The moment he took the scroll, the Four Animals and Twenty-four Elders fell down and worshiped the Lamb. Each had a harp and each had a bowl, a gold bowl filled with incense, the prayers of God's holy people. And they sang a new song:

"Worthy! Take the scroll, open its seals.
Slain! Paying in blood, you bought men and
          women,
Bought them back from all over the earth,
Bought them back for God.
Then you made them a Kingdom, Priests
          for our God,
Priest-kings to rule over the earth."

I looked again. I heard a company of Angels around the Throne, the Animals, and the

Elders — ten thousand times ten thousand their
number, thousand after thousand after thousand
in full song:

> "The slain Lamb is worthy!
> Take the power, the wealth, the wisdom, the
>     strength!
> Take the honor, the glory, the blessing!"

Then I heard every creature in Heaven and earth,
in underworld and sea, join in, all voices in all
places, singing:

> "To the One on the Throne! To the Lamb!
> The blessing, the honor, the glory, the
>     strength,
> For age after age after age."

The Four Animals called out, "Oh, Yes!" The
Elders fell to their knees and worshiped.

## The New Heaven and New Earth

*Revelation 21:1-7*

I saw Heaven and earth new-created. Gone the
first Heaven, gone the first earth, gone the sea.

I saw Holy Jerusalem, new-created, descend-
ing resplendent out of Heaven, as ready for God as
a bride for her husband.

I heard a voice thunder from the Throne: "Look! Look! God has moved into the neighborhood, making his home with men and women! They're his people, he's their God. He'll wipe every tear from their eyes. Death is gone for good— tears gone, crying gone, pain gone—all the first order of things gone." The Enthroned continued, "Look! I'm making everything new. Write it all down—each word dependable and accurate."

Then he said, "It's happened. I'm A to Z. I'm the Beginning, I'm the Conclusion. From Water-of-Life Well I give freely to the thirsty. Conquerors inherit all this. I'll be God to them, they'll be sons and daughters to me."

**Continue the journey. . . . Read the rest of *The Message!***

Maybe you've been reading the Bible for years, or maybe this is your first introduction to it. Regardless of where you are coming from, you will find that *The Message* meets you where you are. *The Message* is written in the same language that you use to write a letter or carry on a conversation with your friends. It is designed to be read like any other book. With no distracting verse numbers or formal language, you'll read chapter after chapter, finding practical insight and wisdom to guide your life.

---

*The Message* is available in many different editions. If you would like a full catalog of Message products, please contact us:

> NavPress
> The Message Catalog
> PO Box 35001
> Colorado Springs, CO 80935

Email:
> the.message@navpress.com

Web site:
> www.navpress.com

---

*The Message* is available at your local bookstore and through Internet booksellers.